Mt. Moiwa, Sapporo, Japan

A TRAVEL PHOTO ART BOOK

LAINE CUNNINGHAM

Mt. Moiwa, Sapporo, Japan

A Travel Photo Art Book

Published by Sun Dogs Creations
Changing the World One Book at a Time
Print ISBN: 978-1-951389-33-8

Cover Image by Laine Cunningham
Cover Design by Angel Leya

Copyright © 2023 Laine Cunningham

All rights reserved. No part of this book may be reproduced in any form or by any means, electronic, mechanical, digital, photocopying or recording, except for the inclusion in a review, without permission in writing from the publisher.

Located in the middle of Sapporo, Mount Moiwa offers a view of the city and, on clear days, the Sea of Japan. A ropeway of gondolas sweeps up to a transfer station where a miniature cable car continues to the top. Hikers who want to tackle the 531-meter climb can start on the longer Asahiyama Park Trail and return via the shorter Jikeikai Hospital route. A rest facility is available at the top.

The 360-degree observation deck looks out over Sapporo and other nearby mountains. A trip taken near dusk sparkles with beauty as the city lights up, making Mt. Moiwa one of the best night views in all of Japan. A top-tier restaurant creates meals that incorporate local flavors and ingredients.

From hours of forest bathing to easy access and spectacular views, Mt. Moiwa has something for everyone.

RODEO

AZURE

HOMESTEAD

BRANCHING

BAMBOO

SWAN LAKE

COASTAL

INBORN

DUNE RUNNER

HELIUM

CONDUCTOR

CURLICUE

STATIC

BIGHORN

ANTIPHONY

SHEAVE

LAMPLIT

TRILLIUM

POPOVER

AUDIENCE

VALLEY

WELCOME

SYNOD

FLASH

CONDUIT

KEEN

SPROUT

OPHIDIAN

RETREAT

GUARDIAN

FARSIGHTED

HALLOWED

WISH

TEMPEST

CHIME

WENDING

BRUSK

VOID

DECOY

REMNANTS

ACTUATE

MOUNTED

TITLES IN THIS SERIES

Gardens of Sapporo, Japan
Mt. Moiwa, Sapporo, Japan
Shinto Temples of Sapporo, Japan
Shrines of Sapporo, Japan
Parks of Sapporo, Japan
Sapporo City, Japan